JOBS ONLINE

HOW TO FIND AND GET HIRED TO A WORK-AT-HOME JOB

LESLIE TRUEX

Copyright © 2011 by Leslie Truex

All rights reserved.

Disclaimer:

This publication is designed to provide information with regard to the subject matter; however, publisher/author is not engaged in rendering legal, accounting or other professional advice. If legal advice or other expert assistance is required, seek the services of a competent professional. Neither the publisher nor author shall be liable for damages arising herefrom.

The fact that an organization or website is referred to in this work as a citation and/or potential source of further information does not mean that the author or the publisher endorses the information the organization or website my provide, or recommendations it may make. Internet resources listed in this work may have changed or disappeared between when this work was written and when it is read.

ISBN-13: 978-1456589189
ISBN-10: 1456589180

About the author

Leslie Truex has been telecommuting and working from home since the early 1990's. Since 1998 she has helped people find or create work-at-home jobs and home businesses through her website WorkAtHomeSuccess.com.

She is the author of The Work-At-Home Success Bible: A Complete Guide for Moms (Adams Media) and teaches work-at-home job courses online and through Piedmont Virginia Community College.

Leslie keeps abreast of the work-at-home job market by searching for and posting work-at-home jobs every weekday on her website and in her weekly newsletter.

She works from home in Central Virginia where she lives with her husband, two children and two cats.

Readers can connect with Leslie through her website, WorkAtHomeSuccess.com, at Twitter @ltruex or Facebook at Facebook.com/leslietruex.

Dedication

To my children for being the inspiration to pursue work at home and to my husband for always supporting my efforts even when they seemed to fail more than they succeeded.

To my mother for always encouraging my endeavors no matter how silly and for being my proofreader. And to my father and step-parents for their love and support.

Finally, this book is for everyone looking to create balance their lives and create a career that they love!

TABLE OF CONTENTS

INTRODUCTION

When I was pregnant with my first child, I thought I would be one of those highly touted supermoms who could work a full day in a job, keep up with housework and still have time and energy to be a wife and mother. But as time went on the image lost its appeal. It was tough enough to get myself ready for work much less get my son ready for daycare. In the evening, housework and bills took what was left of my time and energy. When I had my second child, managing day-to-day tasks became even harder. I began to worry my children were going to grow up without me. So I decided to make money at home.

Like many other people, I researched various work-at-home schemes including envelope stuffing and typing, only to become discouraged at the scams and overpriced information books that didn't provide the information the ads suggested they would. At the time, it didn't occur to me that I already had work-at-home experience. In college I sold kitchen knives. Although I hated selling, I was successful for the two months I was in the knife business. I even earned a free kitchen tool set (which I never received).

After earning my degree, I joined the work force as a social worker and one of my first jobs was in a contract position as an early intervention program coordinator for a rural elementary school. While I was required to be on site for several hours each week, I did most of the paper work and grant writing at home.

Later, I left a full-time on-site position as an adoption social worker to work for the same organization on a contract basis preparing documents and conducting post placement home visits. All this was conducted from my home with visits to the office only to pick up or drop off work.

For some reason, when I thought about finding a working at home job, I didn't think about these experiences. Instead, I did what many work-at-home wannabes do; I answered ads about stuffing envelopes and joined a host of questionable work-at-home schemes and lost money in the process.

My quest to work at home led me to research everything I could about telecommuting on and offline. My goal was to find that one resource that revealed the "secret" to working at home so that I could quit my job. I read just about everything published on the subject of working at home, but no matter how much I read I was disappointed that more details weren't given. Success stories about working at home always started with the person being in debt, coming up with a great work-at-home idea and then they weren't in debt. But what *exactly* did they do to get from debt to no debt? What actions did they take? What did they say and to whom? The details on how to work at home seemed to be one of life's great mysteries.

Fortunately through trial and error I discovered some of the "secrets" and was able to find home-based work in social work, Internet research, writing, and more.

In 1998 I started to share what I'd learned and what I continued to discover about working at home through my website, WorkAtHomeSuccess.com. My goal was to help others avoid the pitfalls and instead, take a more direct path to work-at-home success. While good information about working at home existed, I wanted to provide people with one more step: details to show the way.

Much has changed since 1998. Today it's easier than ever to find work-at-home jobs online. In 1998 I was lucky to find one job a month to post on the website. Today I post 50 jobs each week on the website and email another 20 in the weekly newsletter.

What hasn't changed is that you still can't sign up to type, do data entry or lick envelopes. While work-at-home jobs are prevalent, so are the scams and misinformation that prevent many people from finding legitimate work. This guide will explain what work-at-home jobs are and aren't, as well as how to find them and get hired.

But like all books, the information is just that...information. It doesn't do you any good unless you use it. Throughout the book you'll find worksheets, checklists and resources to help in your job search. Use them. That's what they're there for.

WHAT IS A WORK-AT-HOME JOB?

I'm convinced that the reason people get into trouble when it comes to finding work-at-home jobs is that they don't understand what work-at-home jobs really are. They are misled into believing that they can sign up to type or do surveys. So before I tell you what work-at-home jobs are, let me tell you what they aren't.

Work-at-home jobs are NOT:

- Typing (although you may find a job in transcription)
- Envelope stuffing
- Assembly work
- Data entry (there are a few -- very few-- legitimate data entry jobs).

- Email processing
- Rebate processing
- Transaction processing (or anything that asks you to use your personal bank account or credit card to do business)
- Refund tracer
- Ad placer
- Web surfer
- Survey taker (You can win prizes and sometimes earn a little cash, but it's not a job.)
- Sign-up-do-nothing schemes. This may seem obvious, but I find work-at-home offers all the time that suggest you can make millions just by signing up.

Work-At-Home Jobs

Work-at-home jobs are like any other job; they require skills and experience. You need a quality resume that outlines how you're the best one for the job and go through a hiring process that may include an interview and/or a test.

It may sound daunting, but it's not. If you've ever gotten a job before, you already have the experience needed to get a work-at-home job.

Most Common Work-At-Home Jobs

Finding a legitimate work-at-home job is easy when you look for the right kinds of jobs in the right places. Work-at-home jobs can be found in a variety of fields and organizations. Still, there are some jobs that are more prevalent than others. If you have the skills to do one of the jobs below, your chances of finding work and getting hired are very good. If not, don't get discouraged. This list is not exhaustive.

Customer service

This is one of the fastest growing areas in work-at-home jobs. Big companies such as JetBlue and U-Haul are using home-based workers to help with scheduling and answering customer questions. Other companies use customer service support for order taking.

While some companies require customer service experience, others simply ask that you have a pleasant speaking voice. Many also require that you have high speed internet access and a head-set for your phone.

Transcription (If you want to type, this is the job for you.)

The most common transcription jobs are in medical transcription. While these jobs are abundant, you need training in medical terminology and two or more years of experience. Legal transcription is another area in which you'd need specialized knowledge of legal terms and experience.

General transcription is used by solo entrepreneurs, speakers, coaches and other small businesses that outsource special projects when needed. Or, if you're fast and accurate, captioning is a growing job area in which transcribers type the spoken words from television shows for the hearing impaired.

Aside from the specialized training or knowledge you need for medial or legal transcription, you may also need specific equipment or software. Some companies will supply it while others will require that you purchase it on your own. Watch out for any company that tries to sell its own equipment or software. While legitimate companies will give you a list of resources to find the equipment you need, you want to be wary of a company selling its wares so you can do your job, because more often than not, it will be a scam.

To get the job, you may need to pass a typing test to assess your speed and accuracy.

Virtual Assistant (If you want to do clerical work, this is your job.)

Many small and solo entrepreneurs are now outsourcing their clerical work such as transcribing, correspondence, scheduling and more. Common virtual assistant tasks include checking and responding to email and phone calls, scheduling appointments, updating websites or blogs, writing and submitting advertising, and customer service. Some businesses are looking for virtual assistants with specialized skills such as web page building or bookkeeping, or experience in a specific industry such as real estate.

Most employers will train you on the systems they use, but you'll need to have basic writing skills, knowledge and ownership of software such as word processing, high speed internet access, and the ability to keep up with the boss.

Graphic or web design and web programming

In the past, all the work-at-home jobs outside of sales were related to computers and programming. While there are many jobs in other fields, the opportunities in graphic and web design and programming is plentiful. These jobs require knowledge and experience usually in specific software or programming languages. However, your knowledge doesn't necessarily need to come from a degree or certificate. If you're self taught and have a portfolio, you can find work in this area.

Work can be found in just about every size and type of business and non-profits. You'll need to have a computer that can meet the demands of the job and often specific software such as Photoshop or Quark.

Copywriting, PR and Marketing

It doesn't matter how good a product or service is, if someone doesn't buy it, the company won't make money. So companies rely on words (copywriting) and marketing to get the word out about its products and services. That makes marketing one of the most important jobs there is. The best thing about copywriting and marketing work is that it's extremely lucrative and doesn't necessarily require a degree in advertising.

Copywriting, PR and marketing jobs involve writing ads, brochures, web copy, press releases, and creating and disseminating information for the purpose of marketing a product or service. You can specialize in a specific area such as online marketing, social media marketing or public relations.

Copywriters usually create the written text whether it's a short ad, a long sales letter or a catalog description. If you know desktop or website design, that can be an added bonus to finding work, but it's not required.

Experience more than education is helpful in finding work in copywriting or marketing. People hiring marketing experts want results above everything else. So if you can show you have the goods to entice people to open up their wallets, you have a good chance of finding work.

Sales, Telemarketing, Research

Like technical jobs, work in sales has always been plentiful for the work-at-home wannabe, although few people want to work in sales (I'm in that group as well). But if you are desperate for a job, especially one that can pay very well, then sales may be a good option. Or you can try the less stressful form of telemarketing and do phone surveys. This pays less, but it doesn't require you to badger people.

These jobs sometimes require experience, but usually they just need someone with a computer, phone with a headset, and a thick skin.

Writing

There is a growing need for quality writers especially online. Many small and solo entrepreneurs are hiring writers to create content for their websites and blogs, ghostwrite reports and books, as well as proofread and edit materials. Larger companies are looking for feature or regular content writers to contribute to their websites.

Many writing jobs require an education, but not necessarily in English or journalism. Sometimes a company wants a writer who is knowledgeable about a specific area such as medicine. While you don't need to have a degree in English, you do need to have the skills to research and write a coherent piece.

Tools for writing jobs are a word processing program, a good dictionary and online research resources.

Translation

The world is becoming smaller and smaller. Companies are seeking ways to expand their presence in the world and need to have their websites and other materials translated. Further they are looking for customer service staff who can speak several languages. If you are fluent (speaking and writing) in more than one language, there are many companies that need your services.

Education isn't as important as being fluent in more than one language. But you'll need the skills in the type of work you're doing whether its writing a document or providing customer service.

Other Common Jobs

While these are the most common jobs I find when I search online, there are many others that pop up frequently as well. Some require specific training or licenses.

Accounting/CPA

Auditor

Bookkeeper

Claims Processor

Coder

Data Entry (Excel expert)

Event Planner

Fundraiser

Grant Writer

Illustrator

Indexer

Marketing Experts

Mortgage Originator or Broker

Notary

Nurse

Paralegal Assistant

Public Relations/Marketing

Publicist

Realtor

Researcher

Search Engine Optimization (SEO)

Social Media Marketer

Statistician

Tax preparer

Teacher/Tutor

Travel Agent

Verification Agent

Voice over talent

AVOIDING WORK-AT-HOME SCAMS

"Make Money Stuffing Envelopes!"

"Make Money Reading Email"

"Make Money Assembling Crafts"

These offers sound appealing and often seem too tempting to pass up. Nevertheless, people don't make money from home stuffing envelopes. It is unfortunate that money-grubbing dream stealers have found a niche in scamming people who are looking to work at home. Indeed, millions of Americans spend billions of dollars a year on scams. Some work-at-home schemes sell overpriced information; others teach you how to scam others. Still others send nothing for your money and disappear before you can find them and demand a refund.

Before you send your next $25.00 for start-up materials, take note: EMPLOYERS NEVER CHARGE TO HIRE YOU! Some companies will tell you the money is covering their expenses. Don't believe them. They are selling you something and it isn't a job. After all, you wouldn't pay your employer to set you up on payroll or to supply you with paperclips!

Common scams or deceptive work-at-home ads include:

Typing/Data Entry

"Home Typists Needed."

"Date Entry – No experience necessary."

I used to see these ads and when I'd respond I'd get a pitch to buy an over-priced book on working at home. Now I see these ads online and they are either online versions of envelope stuffing (see below) or affiliate marketing information disguised as a job. Nearly all jobs you run into for typing and data entry will be scams. They will either ask for money (your first tip that it's not a job) or your bank account (fake check scam – see money processing below). Any typing or data entry job that is legitimate will almost always require experience and passing a typing test.

Money/Payment Processing Schemes (fake check scams)

This scam presents itself as a "job" and since it doesn't cost any money to participate, many people are duped into joining and lose thousands of dollars. The scam works like this: A company says it needs help processing payments from customers. You, the "employee" would open or use your personal bank account to deposit "payments" from "customers". Once you have the money, you obtain a certified check made out to the company for the amount deposited into your account minus 10% (your payment). Unfortunately, a few days to a few months later, the bank calls you to inform you that the deposit you made was bogus. You are now responsible for the money you sent in the cashier's check. It is usually thousands of dollars. Not only could you lose your money and banking privileges, but you could be arrested for passing a fake check.

This scam may also be advertised as mystery shopping or customer service. The best way to avoid schemes like this is to remember that *legitimate companies will never ask you to use your personal account in business transactions.*

Envelope Stuffing

Envelope-stuffing ads boast that you can make $400 to $1000 weekly for folding letters or brochures and sealing them in envelopes. The ad asks you to pay a fee to cover expenses or to process your paperwork. What you get for your money are instructions on how to deceive others by placing ads similar to the one you responded to and charging money to teach others how to deceive even more people. In essence, you earn money by duping others into falling for the scheme that you are now perpetuating. Not a very nice way to make a living! And you could get in legal trouble for "scamming" others.

Common sense suggests that envelop stuffing jobs don't make sense. Why would a company in New York pay someone to pack up a box of brochures to mail to Wisconsin to a person who is paid $2.00 for each enveloped stuffed, pay to have it shipped back to New York, and then pay someone to apply postage and mail them? The brochures would have been in the mail twice before even heading to their ultimate destination. Most companies with large mail campaigns use a service that does it all. If not, they do it in house where it is cheaper to use a minimum wage worker.

Assembly Work

Craft assembly work schemes usually require that you spend hundreds of dollars for equipment or supplies, and many hours turning them into miniature dollhouses or other items. The company tells you that it will buy back the finished product from you, but once the work is completed the company refuses to pay you saying your work is not up to its standards or that the product has been discontinued. This scam is all about making money selling you craft kits.

Chain Letters/ Gifting Programs

Remember when a chain letter was a chain letter? It told you to send money, recipes, or whatever to the person on the top of the list and add your name to the bottom. (Then they added a bad luck curse to get you to do it!) Today chain letters have become more clever offering something such as a report in exchange for the money you send. Nevertheless, United States Post Office clearly states that letters that *promise monetary gain*, regardless of what else they offer, are illegal!

According to the United States Postal Inspection Service, a chain letter is a get-rich-quick scheme that promises lots of money by doing what the letter says, which is usually to send cash to the top person on the list and add your name to the bottom. You send the letter to others and eventually your name will move to the top of the list and tons of money will arrive in your mailbox. Sometimes, the letter indicates that you will receive reports for the money you send, and you will send those reports on as you receive money.

The Postal Inspection Service is clear when it says that chain letters, even those that offer some sort of "product" are illegal. "Selling a product doesn't ensure legality. Letters that request money or other items of value, and promise a substantial return to the participants violate Title 18, United States Code, Section 1302, the Postal Lottery Statute." Further, whether the original letter arrives via snail mail, e-mail or any other route, it is still illegal because the U.S. Postal service is used at some point, at least to send the money. (Note: chain letters used to exchange recipes, postcards or other low value items are okay.)

The United States Postal Inspection Service warns people to not be fooled by letters saying the United States Postal services declared it legal. Neither the Postal Service nor the Postal Inspectors give approval to chain letters. It also recommends that you turn any letter you receive that promises money for participation to your local postmaster or nearest Postal Inspector.

More important than legality, chain letters don't work. Many who participate don't send money; they just add their name to the top of the list. Others list numerous names and addresses, but all money goes to one person. And there is no way to get your money back as most require that you send cash. A money chain letter is scam any way you look at it. Don't be taken in.

E-Mail Get Rich Schemes

Are you disappointed when you check your e-mail only to discover scrolling pages of get-rich-quick schemes? Perhaps, in your desire to work at home you have actually read or even responded to one of these ads. The majority of money-making email you receive will be scams and none of it will be a job. Employers don't need to scour the Internet looking for people to hire. Just like in the traditional work world, they post their job announcement and wait for potential employees to apply. So be cautious of any email promising a job or riches.

Other Scams to Watch Out For

While these don't really fall within the realm of home-based jobs, they are scams you may come across:

- Home Business Associations and Home Business Seminars have been investigated by the Federal Trade Commission for misrepresenting earning potentials to consumers. You can visit the Federal Trade Commission online at http://www.ftc.gov to learn more.
- Certain multi-level marketing (MLM) companies are a front for illegal scams or ponzi schemes. You can feel safe with companies like Pampered Chef, Melaleuca and Mary Kay and other established network marketing companies. However, you should always be wary of any company that is new or that you haven't heard of. The distinctions between a legitimate network marketing company and an illegal one include: 1) There are products or services to sell and selling them is necessary to reaping any other benefits such as getting credit for sponsoring others, 2) You can't buy-in at different levels. Everyone starts at the bottom and their work determines their level of achievement, 3) Compensation is clearly described and accurately represented in a written form.

- Just as some network marketing opportunities are scams, so too are some franchise businesses and business opportunities. Visit the Federal Trade Commission (http://www.ftc.gov) for information on business opportunities and franchises.

Protect Yourself

If you feel you have been scammed, you may not get your money, but you can fight back. Use your favorite search engine to find the contact information for the following agencies:

- The State Attorney General's office or the Secretary of State where you live and where the company is headquartered. The staff can tell you if any state laws that regulate business opportunities protect you.
- The Federal Trade Commission. Although the FTC cannot resolve individual disputes, the information you provide may indicate a pattern of possible law violations that the FTC will investigate. Write to the Consumer Response Center, Federal Trade Commission, Washington, DC 20580, call 202-326-2222, TDD 202-326-2502 or visit the FTC online at http://www.ftc.gov.

- The National Fraud Information Center (NFIC) at 1-800-876-7060. NFIC is a nonprofit organization that operates a hotline to provide services and help for consumers who may want to file complaints. NFIC also sends appropriate information to a fraud database maintained by the Federal Trade Commission and the National Association of Attorneys General.

- Your local consumer protection office.

- Your local Better Business Bureau (BBB) and the BBB where the company is located. Visit it online at http://www.bbb.org to find the location of offices.

- Your local Postmaster. The U.S. Postal Service investigates fraudulent mail practices such as chain letters.

FINDING A WORK-AT-HOME JOB

Finding a job takes effort. Finding a work-at-home job is no easier. Many people who search for a home-based job focus on work-at-home ads about typing, envelope stuffing, and assembly work. What they don't realize is that employers with work-at-home options aren't looking for home workers. Like other employers, they are looking for the best-qualified candidate for the position.

The first step in any job hunt is to know what you have to offer an employer. That starts with inventorying your skills and experience. Use the following worksheet to write down all your work, volunteer and other skills and experience that could be used in a job.

When listing all your skills and experience, don't leave anything out, even if it seems insignificant. The virtual work-world is filled with unique, unusual and even fun job types in a host of areas. You never know when all that trivia or knowledge of carburetors will come in handy.

Next use the Skill Sets and Traits check list to mark areas in which you are proficient such as information gathering or project management.

Education and Experience Worksheet

Education	College or School	Dates of Attendance	Degree Earned

Work Experience	Company	Dates of Employment	Duties

Other Experience	Company or Organization	Dates of Experience	Duties Performed

Memberships	Company or Organization	Dates	Information

Licenses, certifications, awards	Company or Organization	Dates	Information

Hobbies and Interests	Experience	Dates	Information

Skill Sets and Traits Checklist

Information Processing	Leadership Skills	Communication Skills
☐ Gathering Information	☐ Managing Projects	☐ Written Communication
☐ Compiling Information	☐ Managing People	☐ Oral Communication
☐ Organizing Information	☐ Initiating Projects	☐ Presentation Skills
☐ Managing Information	☐ Problem Solving	☐ Instructing Skills
☐ Analyzing Information	☐ Initiative	☐ Group Discussion Skills
☐ Assessing Information	☐ Negotiating Skills	☐ Interviewing Skills
☐ Presenting Information	☐ Motivational Skills	

Traits

☐ Adaptable	☐ Discreet	☐ Professional
☐ Assertive	☐ Energetic	☐ Punctual
☐ Competent	☐ Experienced	☐ Reliable
☐ Cooperative	☐ Expert	☐ Resourceful
☐ Creative	☐ Flexible	☐ Responsible
☐ Dependable	☐ Knowledgeable	☐ Self-Motivated
☐ Diligent	☐ Outgoing	☐ Thorough
☐ Diplomatic	☐ Perceptive	☐ Versatile

Identifying Potential Work-At-Home Jobs

The next step is to determine the types of jobs you can do with the skills you have. Using the list of jobs in chapter one, identify the types of industries and positions for which you have the skills and that would be suited to working at home.

Write down jobs and industries here:

_____

_____

_____

_____

_____

This task can be difficult. At this point, you don't know the whole range of jobs that are available to do at home. Most of the jobs I did and still do were not on my list when I first did this activity. While I do the tasks such as research and writing, I didn't have the job type of "Internet researcher" or "Internet content developer " on my list because I didn't know they existed. It's important to recognize that the list of jobs you make may not be the jobs you ultimately find. But it is a start and can help guide you to the job announcements that are appropriate to your skill sets.

Searching for a Work-At-Home Job

Now that you have identified the job skills you have and the types of companies that may need your skills, you need to search for available positions.

Preparing to Search

Before we get to the business of searching for work, you need to get your job search organized. To be honest, I'm organizationally challenged. And I understand that when it comes to organization, it's personal. What keeps me organized may not work for you. However, I'm going to share some tips that you can use or modify to help keep your job materials easy to find and use.

1. **Get a separate email address:** Choose an email that uses your name or a version of your name such as SueSmith@email.com. Many Internet providers allow you to create more than one email address with your account or you can use a free service such as Gmail.

36

Getting a job-search email account does two things: 1) it gives you a professional sounding email (prettykitty@email.com is cute, but not professional) and 2) it can help you organize job search related emails. Plus you can dump it if you start to get job-scam email. Just be sure to give your new employer or potential employers a new email address if you terminate the job search account.

2. **Create a Resume Template:** In the next chapter we will create a resume and discuss how to make it appealing to employers. For now, create a document outlining your skills, education and experience. Create it in a regular word-processing document without any fancy fonts or formats. It will look boring, but in virtual job hunting that is how it's done.

3. **Create a system to track your applications and resume submissions:** This is where you need to determine the best option for you. You can use an Excel sheet or the one provided in this book to put in the details of the job, the date you applied and any notes. Or

you can copy and paste each job announcement into its own document along with your submission date and notes, and save on your computer. In most cases you won't hear back from employers quickly, so having a system of tracking your application can help you know when to follow up.

4. **Make time for your job search:** This is crucial. Too many people try to fit their work-at-home efforts into snippets of time that just happen to become available. But you can't wait for pockets of time to show up. You are probably too busy for that. Instead you need to make time whether it is first thing in the morning, on your lunch break, or giving up reality TV. Once you are organized and know what you are doing, you can speed through an hour of searching and applying for jobs. But you won't search and apply if you don't make the time.

Sample Job Application Tracking Form

Company	Job/Position	Date Sent	Follow-up	Response

Conducting a Search on Job Search Web Sites

I'm going to show you how to find jobs listed as "work at home", but you have to remember that work-at-home jobs are like traditional jobs. If you were looking for work in the traditional world, odds are you wouldn't read every single job announcement in your newspaper. Instead you would scan for the types of jobs you know you are qualified to do. Who cares if there is a work-at-home accounting job if you don't know accounting, right?

Print out and keep your list of skills and experience in front of you as you do your job search. It will guide you to the job types you are qualified to do. For example, if you type fast and know MS Word, jobs such as virtual assistant, personal assistant and administrative support would fit your job skills.

Job Search Sites

There are hundreds of resources for work-at-home jobs. I have supplied a list of over one-hundred job websites you can use on your search. There are three basic types of job search sites;

1) telecommuting databases

2) free general job search sites

3) freelance job sites

Telecommuting Job Databases

Telecommuting databases are the fastest and easiest way to find work-at-home jobs. Further they screen for scams and business opportunities eliminating the need for you to weed them out. The only disadvantage to telecommuting databases is that they cost money. However, I think the expense is worth it for the serious work-at-home job hunter since it saves a great deal of time.

General Job Search Sites

The advantage to general job search sites such as CareerBuilder and Monster.com is that they are free to use and offer many great work-at-home jobs. The trick is to find them. Part of the problem is that scams and business opportunities are posted alongside the jobs. Therefore it is important that you understand how to avoid scams.

When using general job search sites, you need to search for jobs using work-at-home related keywords. I use **"work at home"** (in quotes) and **telecommute** almost exclusively. But other keywords you can use are:

- Contract work
- Freelance work
- Freelance job
- Home-based job
- Home-based work
- Home-based employment
- Telecommute
- Telecommuting
- Telework
- "Work at home"
- "Work from home"

Using these keywords brings up job results that uses these terms, even if they say, "This is not a work at home job". Read the job description to verify it is a work-at-home job.

Once you get your results, many sites let you filter further by selecting categories. This can be a great way to weed out the scams and business opportunities.

> **WARNING - Always be wary of clerical, typing and data entry jobs posted on general job search sites. 99.99% of the time they'll be scams.**

Freelance Job Sites

Freelance jobs sit in the middle between a job and home business. Many businesses hire freelancers for regular, steady work. But freelancers have more flexibility and independence like a home business.

Freelance sites are the best option for finding virtual support type tasks such as typing, transcription and data entry. But you still need to use caution when using freelance sites to avoid being taken by scammers.

Another advantage is that many freelance sites use an auction system. In this system, the freelance site collects the money from the employer upfront to ensure you get paid when the work is completed. When you finish the work and the client is happy, the freelance site pays you.

The challenge of freelance sites that use the auction system is that they aren't free and it can be hard to get your foot in the door. Because your are bidding on projects, you may need to undercut your price to win the bid. But the more work you get and the better your ratings, the more work you can win.

Conducting the Search with Other Online Resources

Job search web sites are not the only resources for finding work-at-home jobs on the Internet. Here are some other resources you can use to search for work-at-home jobs:

- Scan online classified ads for jobs. When reading classified ads, search by the types of jobs or industries that are conducive to working at home such as "bookkeeper". Be careful of scams.
- Pay attention to job announcements posted on the sites you visit for fun or work. The jobs offered by companies with web sites are not always posted in the most visible spot on the web page. Look for links that say "Jobs" or "Employment". Not all jobs listed on the site will be telecommuting jobs. Usually the job announcement will

specify whether or not it can be done at home. If not, e-mail the contact person and ask.

- Search for jobs posted on websites that provide resources to your region. Once you have pulled up a list of web sites highlighting your community, look for links related to careers and employment. You will also find regional job search web sites listed in the appendix.

Warning!

Con artists are not beyond posting their scams on job search sites. If you find a job announcement asking for money, it is not a job. Do not send money to these people no matter how tempting it may be. You can learn more about how to protect yourself from scams in the Avoiding Scams chapter.

Last Thoughts to Keep in Mind

As you begin your work-at-home job search, keep these tips and ideas in mind:

- Abandon the idea that you will find a work-at-home job through the want ads or on the Internet under the heading "Work At Home". Companies with telecommuting programs look for qualified employees to fill the available position. It is the position that is advertised, not the location of the job.

- NEVER PAY MONEY FOR WORK-AT-HOME EMPLOYMENT! Employers do not charge to hire you. Business start-ups require money, but getting hire to a job does not.

- Research the telecommuting phenomenon. The Work-At-Home Success website (www.workathomesuccess.com) can help you.

- There is no rule that you can't have more than one work-at-home job. Combine several part-time contract positions and become a true freelancer! (Note: some companies have a non-compete clause preventing you from working at another company that provides the same type of product or service. Read your contract carefully!).

- If you don't have a skill that is in great demand by companies with work-at-home jobs, learn it. It will increase your chances of finding a work-at-home job. There are many online education resources or you can check your local community college to get the training you need.

- Be flexible. You might not find the perfect situation, but you might find something that meets some of your needs. Take it and use it to gain experience as you search for a better option.

RESUMES THAT GET YOU NOTICED

In the real world as well as in the cyber world, the resume and cover letter are the first chance you have to make an impression on a potential employer. A well-written resume shows that you have the experience and meet the requirements of the job. Further it will help you proceed to the next step in the job hiring process; the interview. A resume that falls short in terms of providing relevant information or lacks professionalism will be discarded. Don't let your resume end up in the reject pile.

Digital Dirt

Before the Internet, people could have secrets lives that the boss or potential employer would never know about. While it is still possible to have a secret life, it can only happen if you don't post it online. Remember that provocative pose in your bikini you posted on Facebook? How about that Tweet full of expletives?

College admission teams and employers use the Internet to learn about you. If you have something posted online that could potentially hurt your chances of getting a job, now is the time to clean it up.

While you can't completely erase your Internet history, you can make it harder for

"But Leslie, it shouldn't matter what I do in my free time."

It shouldn't, but it does. You can argue that it's not fair for an employer to not hire you based on pictures or other materials you posted online for fun. But potential employers look at this material as a representation of your character and if they don't like what they see, they'll hire someone else.

employers to find the stuff you don't want them to see.

1. Start with your social networks by removing photos (and untagging yourself from other people's photos) and comments that could be used against you. If your life

has been a big party, it may be easier to cancel the account and start over with a new one.

2. Do a Google search of your name with and without quotes to see what pops up. If anything scandalous comes up, try to get rid of it by either deleting it or asking the owner of the site it's on to get rid of it.

3. Get the bad stuff ranked lower in the search engines. As mentioned, the Internet never forgets. Even by deleting material, it can still be found online. Using your social networking pages (new or cleaned-up) work on posting positive and responsible sounding content. This will push the old, bad results down in the search engines.

How to Read a Job Announcement

One of the big misconceptions of resumes is that they are simply a listing of your accomplishments. They are actually a marketing document. And what successful marketers know is that you get better results if your materials speak directly to your market. In a job hunt, that means tailoring your resume to fit each job to which you apply. It starts with reading the job announcement to identify the important information needed to create your job-specific resume.

Here are the steps to reading a job announcement and creating a resume that stands out from the crowd:

1) Print the job announcement out or copy and paste it into your word processing program. Not only can you use it to help you create a professional resume, but also you can store it in a binder or online folder to help you track the job and any replies.

2) Circle or highlight all the words that are important to the job. This can include specific knowledge, aptitude, skills, and industry experience. For example, in a virtual assistant job announcement, an employer may ask for knowledge and experience of specific software, minimum typing speed, ability to manage a database, and a home office set up.

3) Match the circled or highlighted items with your skills and experience.

4) Create your cover letter and resume with the circled or highlighted items in mind. Use active verbs and provide specific details that show you are the applicant the employer is looking for. For example, don't just say you know how to use Word. Instead say, "I own and have

used MS Word for ten years to write letters including mail merge, sales materials, and invoices."

5) Don't lie. While you want to match your skills and experience as much as possible to the job announcement, don't embellish or allude to abilities you don't have.

On the next page is an actual job announcement. See if you can identify the important aspects of the job:

Personal Assistant Needed

Looking for a personal assistant with experience either as an Executive Assistant to senior personnel or as an accounting/finance administrator. Position will be working from home or from the home of the employer. Part time (no more than 10-15 hours per week). Acting as a personal assistant to help manage personal items.

Do not apply to this role unless you have:
- 5 years experience minimum
- Exemplary references from Executive level personnel
- Willingness to participate in criminal background check
- Mid level to expert knowledge for online banking and use of Quicken
- Mid level knowledge of Outlook, Google Calendars and other email and calendaring tools
- Understanding and ability to create and organize good filing systems
- Ability to use MacBook and PC systems
- Hands on willingness to schedule and organize personal items (doctors appt, tax consulting, family calendar, family vacations, construction and repair projects around the home)
- Exemplary ability to organize and prioritize tasks and get things done
- Sense of humor and caring/liberal/non-judgmental approach to work and people

The assignment pays $25 per hour (negotiable for the perfect candidate). You will be provided with a PC or MacBook laptop, which remains the property of the employer for the duration of the assignment (but candidate assumes all damage, repair and loss liability). Hours are flexible during Mondays thru Fridays with occasional hours (no more than 2 hours) at weekends. Vacation time is 3 weeks per year unpaid and 1 week per year paid time off. No medical benefits or insurance provided as this is a part time, hourly position.

Only serious candidates should apply.

As you went through this job announcement, what items did you highlight or circle. Did you include:

- 5 years experience minimum
- Exemplary references from Executive level personnel
- Mid level to expert knowledge for online banking and use of Quicken
- Mid level knowledge of Outlook, Google Calendars and other email and calendaring tools
- Understanding and ability to create and organize good filing systems both online and physical
- Ability to use MacBook and PC systems
- Hands on willingness to schedule and organize personal items (doctors appt, tax consulting, family calendar, family vacations, construction and repair projects around the home)
- Exemplary ability to organize and prioritize tasks and get things done
- Sense of humor and caring/liberal/non-judgmental approach to work and people

Match Your Skills to the Job

Once you have a list like this, you want to match your skills and experience to the job. Where did you get your five years of experience? Are any of these resources executive level personal who will give you a reference? Do you know Quicken, Outlook and Google Calendar and for what have you used them? When have you used a PC and a Mac? What experiences do you have that show you are organized?

This may seem like a lot of extra work, but being specific in how your skills match exactly what the employer wants is going to set your resume apart from all the other applicants. While most people are sending in generic applications that are nebulous in the details, your submission will be meeting the employer's specific needs in several if not all areas and therefore making you the perfect candidate for the job.

Look at the following example to see what I mean:

> Virtual Assistant
>
> Part-time position with real estate agent. Must be organized and professional. Ideal candidate will assist agent in typing and data entry (60 wpm), maintaining contact and MLS databases, keeping blog and website up-to-date, e-mail management and search engine submission and Internet marketing.
>
> Knowledge of MS Word, Excel, and basic HTML required. Ability to write clear and concise correspondence is necessary as well. Computer with high-speed Internet access required (no dial-up). Min. high school diploma. Real estate license a plus.

In this example the key items are:

- Real estate

- Organized

- Typing/data entry 60 wpm

- Contact database

- Blog/Website

- SEO and marketing

- Word/Excel/HTML

- Write correspondence

- Computer with high speed internet access

- HS Diploma

Now compare these two cover letters on the next page and decide which the real estate agent will probably want to interview.

To Whom It May Concern, Enclosed is my resume for the job of real estate assistant. Please let me know if you need further information. Sincerely, Jo Job Hunter	Mr. Jones Acme Real Estate Dear Mr. Jones, I'm applying for the job of real estate assistant posted on your website February 12, 2010. Please find my resume outlining my skills and experience below. My database experience will be an asset to your business, as I can manage and update your list of real estate contacts. I also have experience in developing newsletters and other correspondence that can help you keep in touch with your clients and customers. Please let me know if you need any further information. Thank you for your consideration. Julie Job Hunter

Julie Job Hunter matched her job skills to those in the job announcement. As a result, the Realtor is more likely to contact her first.

On the next page you'll find a worksheet to help you match your skills to those required in job announcements you finding during your search.

Job and Skills Matching Worksheet

Job Requirements	Matching Skills
Example: Knowledge of Blogging	Created a blog using Wordpress
Example: Knowledge of Word	Used Word to create letters and mail merge in admin assist job at ABC Co .

Winning Resumes and Cover Letters

Ready to write your resume? Tailoring your cover letter and resume isn't just about matching your skills with the job requirements. It also involves matching your skills to the company and industry overall.

Research

Some job announcements provide details on the company and the job while others provide very little information at all. Either way, doing a little research on the company before submitting your resume can create an even bigger impact, as well as show potential employers that you are resourceful and have research and Internet skills. Compare the two cover letters in the previous section again. If you were the employer, which letter would you respond to first? While Jo Job Hunter provides a generic introduction to a resume, Julie Job Hunter offers so much more. Her letter has provided Mr. Jones with information on how she can specifically help him in his real estate business. Jo may have more experience, but Julie has gained the advantage over Jo because she researched and learned about Mr. Jones's business and how her skills will help him.

To gain the advantage over other applicants, take out the job announcement you found and write down the answers to the following questions:

1. What is the name of the person doing the hiring? This doesn't always appear in a job announcement so you will need to research or even call the company. In the end, you may not find the name, but make a good effort because a letter addresses specifically to the person doing the hiring makes a bigger impression than "To Whom It May Concern".

2. What types of products or services does the company offer and how can your skills and experience help the company with its products and services?

3. What types of customers use the company's services? What experiences do you have with this target market?

4. How is the company owned? Is it a sole proprietorship? A corporation? Public? Private?

5. What is the size of the company? How many employees does it have?

6. Who are the company's competitors? What other companies offer similar products and services?

You can use some of this information on your Job and Skills Matching Sheet. For example, if the company targets small business owners and you once worked with a company that provided services to small business owners, you want to mention this even if the job announcement doesn't specifically ask for this experience.

The best place to start your research is with the company website. The "About" page of a company website offers a great deal of useful information such as the mission statement, history of the company, and past accomplishments. If you aren't able to get the information you need from the company website, e-mail or call the company.

Calling Protocol

Many job announcements will say, "Do not call about this job." If that's the case, be careful about calling. In my experience, a quick call to get the name of the person in charge of hiring is acceptable, but don't press your luck by trying to gather any additional information. Doing so will only make it look like you can't follow directions and possibly annoy the person on the phone who just may be the one in charge of hiring.

Do What You're Told

One of the biggest complaints of online employers is applicants' failure to follow directions. With the delete button one click away, employers don't waste time on applications that don't adhere to the specifications outlined in the announcement.

Following directions seems like a no-brainer. Why wouldn't you follow the directions the company provides for applying to a job? Too often in an attempt to be clever or stand out from the crowd, people break the rules and send a resume with fancy font or other materials the company didn't request. The problem is that sending something other than what is requested indicates that you don't know how to follow directions. The result? No job.

Companies vary on how they want to receive your application or resume. Some have forms online that you can paste your resume into. Others supply an e-mail address. The one rule that is consistent across the board is ***never send your resume as an attachment unless asked to do so.***

Some companies will also want samples of your work. Others will want you to take a test. Always do what is asked. No more and no less.

The Cover Letter

The cover letter is the first thing an employer will read and the key to whether or not your resume will get read. That's a lot of work for a few lines of text. The cover letter or introduction requires a delicate balance of selling yourself without sounding overly conceited. You need to choose your wording and content wisely. In essence, you want to let the employer know in just a few sentences that you are the best candidate for the job.

In the traditional job world, the cover letter is printed on a separate piece of paper than the resume, but when sent by e-mail, the cover letter is an introduction to your resume. The only exception is if your resume is sent as an e-mail attachment (remember to *never* do this unless specifically told to). In this situation, the cover letter is in the body of the e-mail while the resume is attached.

There are four parts to the cover letter:

1. Contact information and salutation: At the top of the page, include your name, address, and date. The salutation should be addressed to a person. Include a title such as Mr., Mrs., Ms., or Dr. Don't refer to the person by their first name.

2. Opening paragraph: Let the hiring personnel know to which position you are applying and where you saw the job announcement. Give a sentence that lets the employer know you have included a resume either in the letter or as an attachment (*only* if the job announcement called for the resume to be sent as an attachment).

3. Brief overview of skills and experience: Highlight the skills and experience you have that meet the job requirements. If you have any skills or experience that exceed the job requirements or have earned any special honors, be sure to indicate that as well.

4. Closing: Your closing should be simple and undemanding. Thank the personnel person for considering your application. Add your closing (e.g., Sincerely) and your name. If you are sending the letter in an e-mail, your name can be directly or one line space below the closing.

Sample Cover Letter

Julie Job Seeker
1111 Oak Lane
City, State, Zip

Date

Mr. Jones, Realtor
XYZ Company
111 Company Lane
City, State, Zip

Dear Mr. Jones,
I am writing in regard to the position of Virtual Assistant
advertised on Internet Jobs on January 1, 2011. Below this
introduction, please find a copy of my resume outlining my
skills and experience.

My Excel database experience will be an asset to your
business as I can manage and update your list of real estate
clients. I also have experience in developing newsletters and
other correspondence using MS Word that can help you keep
in touch with your clients and potential customers.

My other experience includes creating a blog using
Wordpress and HTML, and search engine submission and
Internet marketing strategies that have over 10,000 people
visiting the blog each month.

I appreciate your taking the time to consider my application.
Please let me know if you need any further information or
documentation.

Sincerely,
Julie Job Seeker

Creating Your Resume

You've made it past the delete button and the employer is ready to read your resume. This is another area in which job seekers can easily gain a few extra points by taking the additional time to tailor it to the job. The resume is your first chance to prove you have what it takes to do the job, and can take you to the next step, the interview.

Remember the sample cover letters from Jo and Julie Job Hunter earlier in this lesson? They illustrated the importance of adding details that are specific to the employer. The same is true of your resume. You want to tailor your resume to each job, focusing on the skills and experiences outlined in the job announcement, as well as using bits of information you have learned in your research of the company.

You can use either your word processing program to create the resume or your Notepad accessory (in Windows). The advantage in using your word processing program is that it provides grammar and spelling checks. However, if you use Microsoft Word and plan to e-mail your resume, turn the Smart Quotes feature off as it will turn your quotes and apostrophes into a series of gobbledygook when pasted as text into an e-mail or online form.

Since the majority of online jobs will request your resume in the body of an e-mail, your resume should be written in plain text without any fancy fonts or formatting. Use Times Roman with a 12-point font. Arial is acceptable as well, but avoid other fonts as not all e-mail programs read them correctly. If you are snail mailing your resume, you can opt for more formatting; however, less is more when it comes to the formatting of a resume. Stick to basic fonts and structure.

If you are ready to write, here are six steps to creating a winning resume:

1. In your text editor or word processing program write your name, address, phone number, and e-mail address at the top of the page. You may want to use a P.O. Box, voice-mail number, and secondary e-mail address to help protect your privacy if you plan to post your resume online. Whatever contact information you provide, be sure that you check it regularly.

2. Indicate the job title or objective. In the example above, the job title would be "Virtual Assistant." If you are not applying to a specific position, you can leave this out.

3. Next list your work experience. You don't need to list all your work experience, but you should include work

experience over the last five years starting with your most recent job and working your way back. Include the company, job title, years of work, and an outline of your duties and responsibilities. Remember to describe your work experience with details that fit the job you want.

4. List your education including any courses you have taken after high school whether you graduated from the college or not. Don't forget continuing education courses and other classes you have taken. particularly if they will help you meet the requirements of the job.

5. List your most recent courses first. If you don't have very much work experience, you may want to list your education first.

6. Provide other experience you have that might be relevant to the job such as previous jobs not included above, volunteer experience, internships, licenses or certifications, and association memberships. Again, you may not want to list everything. Choose the experiences that match the requirements for the job.

7. Finally, if you have skills, hobbies, interests, or other information that will help you qualify for the job, list those as well.

Many people add a line about references such as "References are available on request." While you should have a list of references prepared, you don't have to make any mention of it on your resume. An employer will ask you for references if he wants them.

You also do not need to add your social security number to your resume. An employer only needs your social security when you are being hired. By that time you should have investigated the job and employer and an offer of hire.

As you write your resume, use active words to describe your education and experience. Instead of saying, "I did word processing," say, "I type 100 words per minute." Don't use too many adjectives and adverbs. Strong active verbs should be enough to convey your point in the minimum of space that resumes require. See the sample resume on the next page.

Sample Resume

Julie Job Hunter
1111 Oak Lane
Town, State 11111
(111) 555-1111
Julie@jobhunter.com

Objective: Virtual Assistant

Experience:
2004 – 2006 Office Assistant
XYZ Company, City, State
Job Duties: Wrote professional letters and memos using Word. Managed databases using Excel including data merge features into Word. I type 75 words per minute.

Dates Job Title
Company Name, City, State
Job Duties:

Education:
BA College, City, State 1994
Major: English

Other courses:
Beginning and Advanced Excel, City Community College Spring 2001

Awards and Associations:
Worker of the Year 2003 and 2005
Member of International Virtual Assistant Association 2008 to present.

Other Experience:
Created blog using Wordpress and HTML. Speak fluent Spanish.

Resume Checklist

Before sending your resume and cover letter to a potential employer, check to make sure you have met all the important requirements of a winning resume:

___ State only those skills and experiences that fit the specific job.

___ Tailor the resume and cover letter to the specific job.

___ Use a professional tone.

___ Share only the skills you have.

___ Share your knowledge, but don't brag or exaggerate.

___ Be honest.

___ Give only the information the job announcement requests.

___ Refer to yourself as "I."

___ Have perfect grammar and spelling. Read and reread. Better yet, have someone you trust proof your resume and cover letter for errors.

Waiting to Hear Back

One of the biggest challenges to getting a work-at-home job is waiting for a response to your resume. In many, if not most cases, you won't hear back at all. The frustrating part is that by not hearing back, you have no feedback about why your resume is not being considered or how you can improve it.

There are several reasons you don't hear back from an employer:

1. You don't have the skills or experience the employer wants.
2. You didn't follow the instructions for applying.
3. The job announcement is old and the company has enough applicants, but hasn't removed the announcement.
4. The employer is overwhelmed with applications and is taking a long time to respond.
5. The resume is lost in cyber-space.

Following-up with an employer is recommended, but needs to be done carefully. If the job announcement specifically says not to call, then don't call. If it has a closing date for accepting applications, wait a week after the deadline and email to verify receipt of your resume. If no close date is given, email a week after you've submitted your application to verify it was received. If you don't hear back, wait another week to call, unless the job announcement says not to call.

If you still aren't hearing back, verify that you have the skills and experience for the jobs to which you are applying. Ask a friend or hire a resume service to review your resume to make sure it does you justice.

Another way to improve your marketability is to get more training. Today universities and community colleges are offering home-based online courses that can beef up your skills and help you become more appealing to employers.

Finally, ABA or Always Be Applying. Don't submit a resume and then sit back and wait for a response. As I've already mentioned, in most cases you won't hear back. Instead, search and apply for jobs daily until you get hired.

The Interview

Depending on the job, you may not have an interview at all. Some jobs will want a phone interview, while others will have a questionnaire. And some will want samples of your work in lieu of an interview.

Whatever sort of interview or screening process the employer uses, focus on your skills and experience and not on your desire to work at home. Like all other jobs, the employer with a work-at-home job is looking for the best candidate to fill a position. He may be sympathetic to your financial plight, but won't hire you because of it.

The interview is about selling yourself to the hiring person. Communicate how you can be an asset to the company. Be positive about yourself, previous jobs and the company to which you are applying. Always be professional and make a good impression.

EMPLOYMENT STATUS AND CONTRACTS

In the work at home world not all jobs come with the status of "employee". That doesn't mean that work isn't regular or ongoing. It just means that companies prefer to take on workers in a contract or freelance status. It saves them money and it could save you a bundle in taxes as well. (Note: I'm not a tax expert, so please consult with a tax professional about contract and freelance work tax benefits.)

The distinction between an employee and a contract worker is an important one. Not only does it affect the relationship between the company and worker, it can have tax implications as well. An *employee* is a worker who is hired full or part-time, is paid a salary or hourly wage, often receives benefits, and whose employer deducts tax and social security. A *contract worker* differs in that an organization makes a contract with the worker to complete specific tasks or projects. While contract workers can be "hired" for full or part-time work, they are usually paid when certain tasks or projects are completed. Further, the contracting organization pays the worker a straight fee or commission without tax or social security deductions.

There are exceptions and gray areas in the definitions of employee and contract worker. Because of this, it is important to know before you accept a job how you are going to be categorized by the company and whether or not it will be issuing a W-2 (employee earnings) or 1099 (contract work payments) for tax purposes.

Which is better? Both have their advantages and disadvantages. Employee status offers the security of a stable (maybe) job, a regular paycheck and sometimes benefits. On the other hand, workdays and hours may not be flexible. Further, employees may be required to work on site a set number of days per week or month. And frequently, employees need to live within a certain mile or time radius of the company site to attend meetings or other company-related events.

Contract work usually offers the flexibility of setting one's own schedule. Because work is project-based, contract workers can work at a tempo that earns them the income they desire. If they want to earn a specific amount of money and can meet the requirements needed to earn it, they can. They aren't limited by a set salary or wage. On the other hand, they only earn when they produce.

Another factor in contract work is paying one's own taxes. While you can deduct expenses such as mileage, supplies, your internet connection and maybe even a portion of your housing costs, coming up with money at tax time can be difficult and frustrating if money isn't set aside in advance.

Those wanting to work at home will find many more contract jobs than salaried jobs. The companies paying salary and benefits to telecommuters are generally in areas requiring highly skilled or experienced workers. But don't let that scare you away from finding a work-at-home job. Work opportunities are abundant and with a little planning, you may end up earning more money and having more tax advantages, while working fewer hours.

Employment Contracts

Before taking any work-at-home job, get all the terms in writing. Most companies will automatically give you a contract that outlines all the terms of job. If it doesn't, ask for one. Without a contract, you have no recourse if the company fails to pay you. The contract should cover:

- The company and individuals involved
- What the work entails
- Wage or salary and payment schedule
- Days and times you are expected to work if required by the company
- Date the job will start
- Probationary period
- Address of the remote (your) office
- Any equipment the company will be supplying
- Equipment the company expects you to have
- Potential expenses (i.e. travel, long distance calls, etc.) and who will cover them
- Childcare arrangements if a concern to the employer
- Contact information for all parties such as phone, e-mail, fax etc.
- Reporting methods and schedules
- Any other issues you or the employer deem relevant.

FINAL THOUGHTS

Work-at-home jobs allow you the flexibility to balance your personal and work life. But like any other job, you are required to fulfill your end of the deal by performing quality work. One of the biggest challenges people have when they first start working at home is creating the balance and structure needed to live and work under one roof. Some people get distracted by children, laundry or the ability to go out to lunch with friends, and don't work. Others work all the time. Here are some tips to avoid these problems:

1. Treat your work-at-home job the same as you would a traditional job. Be profession and hard working.

2. Keep in touch with your employer and colleagues to stay in the loop.

3. Set up a home office that is separate from other areas of the home. Ideally it should have a door, good lighting and a comfortable chair.
4. Create a work schedule. Show up and clock out on time.
5. Have all your materials and to-do list ready when you sit down to work.
6. Learn to say 'no' to neighbors, friends and family who want you to do favors 'since you're at home' or want to socialize. Let them know your schedule.

JOB SEARCH WEBSITES

Websites that List Telecommuting Jobs

The sites below list work-at-home jobs. Most of these resources are free. Thos marked with $ have a fee to access their work-at-home job database. Please review the scam information as sometimes scams or non-job opportunities can get listed on the free websites.

2Work-At-Home.com *http://www.2work-at-home.com*

FlexJobs $ *http://www.flexjobs.com*

HomeJobStop $ *http://www.homejobstop.com*

Rat Race Rebellion *http://www.ratracerebellion.com*

VirtualAssistance.com $ *http://www.virtualassistants.com/*

WAHM *http://www.wahm.com/jobs.html*

Work-At-Home Success *http://www.workathomesuccess.com*

Freelance Job Resources

General Freelance Work

Elance ($) *http://www.elance.com*

Guru *http://www.guru.com*

HomeworkersNet
http://www.homeworkersnet.com/job_listings.php

Workaholics4Hire *http://www.workaholics4hire.com/main.htm*

Freelance Job Resources—Computer and IT Work

Computer Jobs *http://www.computerjobs.com/homepage.aspx*

Contract Job Hunter *http://www.cjhunter.com*

Dice *http://www.dice.com/*

JustTechJobs *http://www.justtechjobs.com/Gateway.asp*

Planet Recruit *http://www.planetrecruit.com/channel/int* Search
using "Freelance."

Project Spring ($)
http://www.projectspring.com/freelance/index.html

Rent a Coder
http://www.rentacoder.com/RentACoder/default.asp

Freelance Writing Work

Absolute Writers *http://www.absolutewrite.com/Markets.htm*

Avalanche of Jobs *http://www.sunoasis.com*

Freelance Writing *http://www.freelancewriting.com/freelance-writing-jobs.php*

MediaBisto *http://www.mediabistro.com*

MTjobs *http://www.mtjobs.com/*

ProBlogger *http://jobs.problogger.net*

WritersWeekly.com *http://www.writersweekly.com*

General Job Search Web sites

These sites offer general job announcements. Once you access the Web site, use keywords such as "telecommute" and "work at home" to search the databases.

United States Job Search web sites

6 Figure Jobs *http://www.6figurejobs.com*

AdQuest3-D

http://www.adquest3d.com/search/search.asp?BRD=1&PAG=8 7

CareerBuilder Network *http://www.careerbuilder.com*

Career Journal from the Wall Street Journal

http://www.careerjournal.com/

Employment911 *http://www.employment911.com*

Flipdog *http://www.flipdog.com*
Job.com *http://www.job.com/my.job*
Jobs.com *http://www.jobs.com/*
Job Central *http://www.jobcentral.com/*
JobHunt *http://www.job-hunt.org*
KellyCareerNetwork *http://jobsearch.kellycareernetwork.com/*
Monster.com *http://www.monster.com*
Net-Temps *http://www.net-temps.com*
True Careers *http://www.truecareers.com*
WorkTree.com $ *http://www.worktree.com/*
Yahoo HotJobs *http://www.hotjobs.com/*

Regional Northeast Job Search Web sites
Boston Works *http://bostonworks.boston.com/*
Boston Job Bank *http://www.bostonjobs.com*
Find It Online *http://www.finditonline.com/400.htm*
New Jersey Online *http://www.nj.com/jobs/*
Philadelphia Job Net *http://www.jobnet.com*
TriState Jobs
http://www.tristatejobs.com/ad_local_search.html#dup0

85

Regional Midwest Job Search Web sites

Career Board *http://www.careerboard.com/*

Minnesota Jobs *http://www.minnesotajobs.com/*

Online Columbia

http://www.onlinecolumbia.com/jobsearch.asp

Regional South and Southeast Job Search Web sites

Florida Career Link *http://www.floridacareerlink.com*

Triangle Jobs *http://www.triangle.com/#*

Regional West Job Search Web sites

Alaska Job Center *http://www.ilovealaska.com/alaskajobs/*

Bay Area Jobs *http://www.bajobs.com*

Colorado Jobs *http://www.coloradojobs.com/*

Oregon Employment Department

http://www.emp.state.or.us/empmtsvcs/

Work Source Washington

http://www.wa.gov/esd/employment.html

Canadian Job Search Sites

Actual Jobs Canada *http://www.actualjobs.com/search/can.html*

Innovisions Canada *http://www.ivc.ca/*

Work Search *http://worksearch.gc.ca*

COMPANIES THAT FREQUENTLY TAKE APPLICATIONS

Where possible I have provided links directly to the job information page. However, some pages require you to click on a link from the home page. For those listings you'll see directions on what to click.

Websites are updated and changed frequently and you may find that some links to the career pages don't work. If that is the case, access the main site (eliminate the page address and instead go to the main domain ie: if it is abc.com/careers.html that isn't working, go to abc.com and see if there is a link to careers from there).

Some companies hire both home-based and onsite staff so you will need to read the job information carefully to identify the telecommuting opportunities.

I cannot guarantee that these companies are hiring right now or that they provide steady, ongoing work. These companies indicate on their websites that they accept applications ongoing. With that said, you will need to meet the requirements the companies outline for being considered for work.

Administrative Support/Virtual Assistants/Data Entry/General Transcription/Captioning

Absolute Docs *http://www.absolutedocs.com/careers.htm*

AccuTran Global *http://www.accutranglobal.com/jobs.html*

Alderson Reporting
http://www.aldersonreporting.com/Jobopps/courtrep.asp

Alice Darling Secretarial Services, Inc
http://www.alicedarling.com/about/employment.html

American High Tech Transcription
http://www.htsteno.com/employment.html

Axion Data *http://www.axiondata.com/employreq.htm*

Cambridge Transcription
http://www.ctran.com/employment.html

Capital Typing *http://www.capitaltyping.com/employment-application*

Caption Colorado *http://www.captioncolorado.com/available-job-opportunities*

Continental Promotion Group *http://www.cpginc.com/*

CyberDictate
http://www.cyberdictate.com/company/employment/

Dion Data Solutions
http://www.diondatasolutions.net/opportunities.htm

Diversified Reporting
http://www.diversifiedreporting.com/job.html

DriverGuide.com (database entry of device drivers)
http://www.driverguide.com/hiring.htm

Edge Virtual Assistance (The) *http://www.the-edge-va.com/about/want-to-join-our-team/*

eScriptionists *http://www.escriptionist.com/employment.htm*

eTranscription Solutions
http://www.etranscriptionsolutions.org/careers.php

ExecuScribe *http://www.execuscribe.com/index.php?q=node/6*

Expedict *http://www.expedict.co.uk/work.php*

Express Document Service, Inc
http://www.expressdocumentservice.com/jobs.html

Fantastic Transcripts
http://www.fantastictranscripts.com/workhome.htm

Mass Transcription
http://www.masstranscription.com/employment.php

Morningside Partners *http://www.fdch.com/careers.htm*

Mountain West Processing
http://www.mountainwestprocessing.com/page5.html

Mulberry Studio *http://www.mulberrystudio.com/jobs.htm*

Net Transcripts
http://www.nettranscripts.com/nt_employment.htm

Office Team *http://www.officeteam.com/*

Palm Coast Data (Palm Coast Florida Residents)
http://www.palmcoastdata.com/careers/work-from-home-florida/

Production Transcripts
http://www.productiontranscripts.com/jobs.php

Purple Shark *http://www.thepurpleshark.com/index.html*

SpeakWrite
http://typist.youdictate.com/TypistNav/employment.htm

TASK Transcription *http://usetask.com/description.html*

Team Double Click
http://www.teamdoubleclick.com/Current_Openings.html

Tigerfish (trsanscription)
http://www.tigerfish.com/employment.html

Transcription 2000 *http://www.transcription-services.org/request-employment.php*

Transcription Studio *http://www.transcriptionstudio.com/transcribers.htm*

TruTranscripts *http://www.trutranscripts.com/transcription-jobs.htm*

Ubiqus Reporting *http://www.ubiqus.com/*

Viable Technologies (transcription) *http://www.viabletechnologies.com/jobs.php*

Virtual Assistants *http://www.virtualassistantjobs.com/duties.html*

VITAC Real Time Captioning *http://www.vitac.com/careers/index.asp*

Wordz Xpressed *http://www.wordzx.com/ContactUs.html*

Working Solutions *http://www.workingsol.com/agents_page/*

Accounting/Bookkeeping/Financial/Real Estate

Accountants International *http://www.accountantsintl.com/*

American Title Inc *http://www.americantitleinc.com/static/emp.asp*

Balance Your Books *http://www.balanceyourbooks.com/jobs.shtml*

Bateman & Co. Inc, P.C. (click on employment)

http://www.batemanhouston.com/

Bookminders (need to live in S. PA)

http://www.bookminders.com/careers/index.html

Click Accounts

http://www.clickaccounts.com/whoweare_careers.html

ClickNWork

http://www.clicknwork.com/opportunities/analysts/

Dotun and Casserly *http://www.dcfsi.com/careers.htm*

Jelly Bean Services (mortgage loan processors)

http://work4jbs.com/jbs/apply.htm

Nationwide Loan Processors

http://www.loanprocessor.org/work-at-home-job-opportunities.html

OSI Business Services *http://www.osibusinessservices.com/*

Tad Accounting *http://www.tadaccounting.com/careers.html*

Total Business Care

http://www.totalbizcare.com/opportunities.htm

VT Audit *http://www.vtaudit.com/careers.asp*

Warrener Stewart http://*www.warrenerstewart.com/recruit.html*

Communities Guides / Experts / Consultants

About.com *http://beaguide.about.com*

Bella Online *http://www.bellaonline.com/misc/joinus/index.asp*

Cha Cha Guide *http://search.chacha.com/guidesignupnow*

Clarity Consultants *http://www.clarityconsultants.com/why-work-with-us.asp*

Dissertation Advisors
http:*//www.dissertationadvisors.com/consulting.shtml*

Guideline *http://www.opinionresearch.com/careers.shtml*

Just Answer *http://www.justanswer.com/expert.aspx*

Live Person *https://www.liveperson.com/registration/expert-registration/expert-signup.aspx*

National Seminars Training
http://www.nationalseminarstraining.com/CareerOpps/Career Opps.html

Customer Service/Teleservices

1-800Contacts *https://jobs.1800contacts.com/careers/index.asp*

1-800Flowers
http://ww10.1800flowers.com/template.do?id=template8&page =9000#1

27/7 In Touch (Canada) *http://www.24-7intouch.com/career_opportunities.htm*

AAA Renewals *http://www.aaarenewals.com/i_careers_RS.htm*

Accolade Support *http://www.accoladesupport.com/techjob.html*

AccuConference *http://www.accuconference.com/careers.html*

ACD Direct *http://acddirect.com/becomeanagent.html*

Advanis *http://www.advanis.ca/Corporate/Careers*

Affina *http://affinahomeagent.com/*

Alpine Access *http://www.alpineaccess.com/external/careers/become_an_agent.html*

American Airlines *http://www.aacareers.com/us/frame_index.htm?http&&&www.aacareers.com/us/index.shtml*

Ansafone Communications *http://www.ansafone.com/Employment.aspx*

APAC Customer Service http://*www.apaccustomerservices.com/careers/index.cfm?id=1 00*

Arise *http://www.arise.com/work-at-home/*

ARO Business Process Outsourcing
http://www.callcenteroptions.com/careers.asp

Auralog *http://tmm.catsone.com/careers/index.php*

Blue Zebra
http://www.bluezebraappointmentsetting.com/Careers.aspx

Call Center International *http://www.ccicompany.us/*

Call Center Options *http://callcenteroptions.com/*

Channel Blend *http://www.channelblend.com/app_intro.php*

Cloud 10 Corporation *http://www.cloud10corp.com/*

Connect2Agent
http://www.connect2agent.com/c2aplus/careers.asp

Convergys *http://206.126.172.177/*

Customer Loyalty Concepts
http://www.customloyal.com/Employment.aspx

Customer Service Review *http://www.csr-net.com/jointeam.htm*

DeRosa *http://www.derosa.com/callteam.htm*

eCallogy *http://www.ecallogy.com/careers.html*

Expert Business Development
http://www.expertbizdev.com/join_our_team.htm

Extended Presence
http://*www.extendedpresence.com/salesjobs/JobDescription.asp*
?JID=51

GE Call Centers *http://www.gecallcentercareers.com/*

Grindstone *http://www.grindstone.com/career.html*

Hire Point *http://www.hirepoint.com/athome/index.html*

Hilton Reservations *http://hrccjobs.com/*

HSN *http://www.hsn.com/careers_at-988_xa.aspx?nolnav=1&o=!BNJO0&cm_sp=Global*BN*Care ers*

ICT Group / Sykes *http://www.ictgroup.com/careers.aspx*

InfoCision *http://www.infocision.com/Careers/Pages/WorkFromHome.aspx*

JLodge *http://www.jlodge.com/*

JetBlue *http://www.jetblue.com/about/work/*

LiveOps *http://agentcommunity.liveops.com/index.html*

Lunar Pages *http://www.lunarpages.com/jobs/*

Medco *https://www.medcohealth.apply2jobs.com/*

MicahTek, Inc *http://www.micahtek.com/jobs.shtml*

N.E.W. *http://www.newhomebasedccr.com/ccrfaqs.asp*

Next Level Solutions *http://www.dial-nls.com/content.php?link=Careers_ind*

O'Currance Teleservices *http://www.ocurrance.com/employment.php*

OnPoint Advocacy *http://www.onpointathome.com/*

Prince Market Research *http://pmresearch.com/employment*

Progressive Business Publications
http://www.pbp.com/employment.asp

Public Opinion Research
http://www.publicopinionresearch.net/apply/

SCI Live *http://www.scilive.com/call-center-careers.htm*

Service 800 *http://www.service800.com/2/careers.aspx*

Sutherland At Home *http://www.sutherlandathome.com/*

TeLCare *http://www.telcarecorp.com/about-us/career-opportunities*

The Call Center Inc
http://www.thecallcenterinc.com/contactUs/careers.asp

Time Communications
http://www.timecommunications.biz/comp_employment.asp

U-Haul
http://jobs.uhaul.com/job_detail.aspx?aval_job_id=68659&mode=

Ver-A-Fast *http://www.verafast.com/job_opportunities.htm*

VIP Desk *http://www.vipdesk.com/info/default.asp*

Voice Log *http://www.voicelog.com/careers.html*

West At Home *http://apply.westathome.com/*

Westat
*https://sjobs.brassring.com/en/asp/tg/cim_advsearch.asp?partn
erid=82&siteid=5197*

Working Solutions *http://www.workingsol.com/agents_page/*

XAct Services *http://www.xactservices.com/company/careers/*

Disabled Employees
Barrier Free Choices
http://www.barrierfreechoices.com/careers/

Lift, Inc *http://www.lift-inc.org/apply.html*

NTI Central *http://www.nticentral.org/apply/a0030OLD.shtm*

Human Resources/Recruiting
Career Search Consultants *http://www.cscrecruiters.com/*

Dierdra Moire Corporation
*http.//www.diedremoire.com/main.asp?uri=1060&mn=13&sti
=256*

EEG Recruiting
*http://www.eegrecruiting.com/JoinOurTeam/tabid/57/Default.a
spx*

Enid, Chesterfield and Co.
http://www.enidchesterfield.com/career.php

Healthcare Recruiters International

http://www.hcrintl.com/default.cfm?page=113

HR Advice *http://www.hradvice.com/contact.html*

IRES, Inc *http://www.iresinc.com/recruitercareers/*

Pioneer Staffing

http://www.pioneerstaffing.com/careersAtPioneer.html

Law/Legal Transcription/Mock Juror Jobs

Cambridge Transcription

http://www.ctran.com/employment.html

Counsel On Call

http://counseloncall.com/Page/Job_Opportunities

CyberDictate

http://www.cyberdictate.com/company/employment/

eJury (mock juror)

http://www.ejury.com/jurors_learn_about.html

eTypist *http://e-typist.com/Employment_work_at_home-dictation-service.htm*

Hire Counsel *http://www.hirecounsel.com/jobs_landing.php*

Jelly Bean Services *http://work4jbs.com/jbs/apply.htm*

Jury Test (mock jurors)

http://www.jurytest.com/index.cfm?action=howjur

Mass Transcription

http://www.masstranscription.com/employment.php

MicroMash Bar Review (click on Apply to be a Mentor)

http://www.micromashbar.com

Online Verdict (mock jurors)

http://www.onlineverdict.com/jurors.php

Neal R. Gross *http://www.nealrgross.com/employment.htm*

Real Solutions LCC (real estate closings)

http://www.clicknclose.net/Join_20_HomeNetwork.html

SPI *http://www.spi-bpo.com/web/spi/apply.jsp?fldr_id=384&service=_Show_All*

TASK Transcription *http://usetask.com/description.html*

Trial Juries (mock jurors)

http://www.trialjuries.com/trialjuries/pub/jurors/signup/j_sign.l asso

Trial Practices (mock jurors)

http://www.trialpractice.com/juror.htm

TypeWrite (legal transcription) *http://typewp.com/default.html*

Medical / Nursing (not including medical transcription or coding)

Doctors On Demand

http://docond.com/Common/Physicians/ApplyNow.aspx

Fonemed *http://www.fonemed.com/jobs/index.html*

Imaging On Call

http://www.imagingoncall.net/secondary/careers.aspx

Medzilla (job search) *http://www.medzilla.com/findjobs.html*

United Health Group *http://careers.unitedhealthgroup.com/*

Virtual Radiologic

http://tbe.taleo.net/NA7/ats/careers/jobSearch.jsp?org=VIRTU ALRADIOLOGIC&cws=1

Medical Transcription and Coding

Accurate Typing Services

http://www.accuratetyping.net/employment.html

AccuScribe *http://accuscribe.net*

AccuTran Global *http://www.accutranglobal.com/jobs.html*

Advanced Transcription

http://www.advancedtx.com/employment.php

American Transcription Solutions *http://atsi-inc.com/Careers.asp*

Amphion Medical

http://www.amphionmedical.com/html/careers.php

Applied Medical Services

http://www.appliedmedicalservices.com/career_main.html

Arrendale Associates, Inc

http://www.aaita.com/position_available.html

Ascend Health Care

http://www.ascendhealthcare.com/employment.html

Aviacode

http://www.aviacode.com/MedicalCoding/?Page=Careers

CCS Transcription

http://www.ccstranscription.com/applyjobs.html

Code Busters (click on Join Us) *http://codebusters.com/*

Complete Coding Solutions

http://www.completecodingsolutions.com/jobs.html

DSG Medical Transcription Solutions *http://www.dsg-inc.net/careers.aspx*

EFD Transcription Service

http://www.efdtrans.com/opportunities.htm

Expedite (British Columbia, Canada) *https://www.expedite-transcription.com/contact.htm*

ExecuScribe *http://www.execuscribe.com/team.htm*

Express Document Services, Inc
http://www.expressdocumentservice.com/jobs.html

Focus Infomatics *http://www.focusinfomatics.com/careers.htm*

LexiCode *http://www.lexicode.com/remoteathome.html*

Mag Mutual *http://www.magmutual.com/careers.html*

MD-IT *http://www.md-it.com/contact-employment*

MediGrafix *http://medigrafix.com/Opportunities/*

MedQuist
http://www.medquist.com/Home/SolutionsServices/tabid/56/Default.aspx

MXSecure *http://www.mxsecure.com/careers/index.htm*

NJPR *http://www.njpr.com/employment.html*

Oracle Transcription
http://www.oracleti.com/medical-digital-transcription-careers/medical-transcriptionist.html

Outsourcing Solutions, Inc
http://www.ositranscription.com/recruiting.html

Perfect Transcription
http://*www.nealrgross.com/employment.htm*

Personal Touch Coding Solutions
http://www.personaltouchcoding.com/careers.htm

Phoenix Medcom

http://www.phoenixmedcom.com/requirements.htm

Precyse Solutions (type "work at home" in the search box)

https://precysesolutions.tms.hrdepartment.com/cgi-bin/a/searchjobs_quick.cgi

Presynct Technologies, Inc

http://www.presynct.com/careers.html

Professional Medical Services, Inc

http://www.professionalmedicalservices.org/mt_requirements.html

ScribeCare (scroll down to Career)

http://www.scribecare.com/web/content/blogcategory/15/43/

Skilled Transcription Services *http://ststranscription.com/*

SpectraMedi *http://www.spectramedi.com/medical-transcription-services-jobopening.htm*

Spheris *http://www.spheris.com/careers/*

SPI *http://www.spi-bpo.com/web/spi/landing.jsp?fldr_id=397&service=_Show_All*

StatIQ Solutions *http://www.statiq.com/careers.html*

StenoMed, Inc *http://www.stenomed.com/careers.htm*

SuperScript Medical Transcription

http://www.superscriptmedical.com/subcontractors.html

The Coding Network *http://www.codingnetwork.com/jobs.html*

Thomas Transcription

http://www.thomastx.com/application.php

Torres-Lich & Assoc. Inc *http://www.torres-lich.com/Employment.htm*

Transcend

http://www.transcendservices.com/Corporate/careers_MLSrequ irements.asp

TransHealth *http://www.transhealth.com/employment.htm*

Trans Tech Medical Solutions

http://www.transtechmedical.com/careers.html

TRX *http://www.trxinc.net/transcription-careers.aspx*

Ubiquis (click on Working for Ubiquis) *http://www.ubiqus.com/*

United Medical Transcription *http://www.unitedtr.com/*

Miscellaneous Jobs (jobs that don't fit into another category)

Aria (card writing) St. Cloud, MN

http://www.ariacallsandcards.com/positions/writejob2.htm

Cherry Lane Music Co. (guitar transcribers, piano arrangers, educational writers) *http://www.cherrylane.com/clprint/About-Us/Employment-Opportunities.aspx*

EBI (background screening)

http://www.ebiinc.com/background-investigation-careers.html

Face the World (student exchange rep)

http://www.facetheworld.org/jobop.html

Hausernet (mail decoy)

http://www.hausernet.com/opportunities.html

Opuzz Voice (voice talent) *http://www.opuzzvoice.com/*

RecruitZone (athletic recruiting)

http://www.recruitzone.com/become_scout.asp

Write On (hand writing) Fredrick,MD

http://www.writeonresults.com/?page_id=9

Notary Jobs

AES Title *http://www.aestitle.com/contact.html*

American Signing Connection, LLC

http://www.americansigningconnection.com/index.html

American Title Inc

http://www.americantitleinc.com/static/emp.asp

CDS Signing *http://www.cdssigning.com/index.php*

Signing Source Inc

http://www.signingsource.com/p_notaries.asp

Vital Signing Inc *http://www.vitalsigning.com/notary.html*

PR/Marketing

Partner Centric (Internet marketing)

http://www.partnercentric.com/careers/

Research Jobs

AB Check Court Researcher *http://abcheck.com/researcher.asp*

Accurate Background (court researchers)

https://www.accuratebackground.com/contact/research.htm

Background Profiles (court researchers)

http://www.backgroundprofiles.com/

Clicknwork *http://www.clicknwork.com/opportunities/*

Harvey E. Morse, P.A.

http://www.probate.com/current/employment/employment_cont

ent.htm

Information Technologies (court abstractors/data collectors)

http://www.inft.net/general/employment.htm

JellyBean Services http://work4jbs.com/jbs/apply.htm

National Background Screening (court researchers)

http://www.validityscreening.com/Employment

Sunlark Resarch (court researchers)

http://www.sunlarkresearch.com/researchers.htm

United Data Network (court researchers)
http://www.uniteddatanetwork.com/work.htm

Yahoo *http://promo.yahoo.com/user_research/*

Sales/Appointment Setting/Telemarketing/Fundraising

Arise *http://www.arise.com/work-at-home/*

Blue Zebra Appointment Setting
http://bluezebraappointmentsetting.com/Careers.aspx

Cruise.com
http://www.cruise.com/misc_pages/employment.asp?skin=001&pin=&phone=888-333-3116

Extended Presence *http://extendedpresence.com/joblisting.asp*

Grindstone *http://www.grindstone.com/career.html*

Great American Opportunities (fundraising sales)
http://www.gafundraising.com/careerOpportunities.php

TelereachJobs *http://telereachjobs.com/*

Telexpertise
http://telexpertise.com/work_at_home_jobs_telephone.html

Translation, Interpreter, and Language Services

ABC Translation Services

http://www.translationsabc.com/career-opportunities.php

Accurapid Translation

http://accurapid.com/accurapid/xlatorfr.html

African Translation

http://www.africatranslation.com/Translators.html

Berlitz

http://careerservices.berlitz.com/current_job_vacancies.asp

Bilingva *http://www.bilingva.com/careers.html*

Bridge Linguatec *https://www.bridgelinguatec.com/careers.php*

Butler Hill Group *http://www.butlerhill.com/job/index.html*

Creative English Solutions (Canada)

http://www.englishsolutions.ca/ces_jobs.php?set_lang=en

Dialog One *http://www.dialog-one.com/opportunities.html*

Global Link Translation

*http://www.globalinktranslations.com/work_with_us.asp?sectio
n=workwithus*

Japan Pacific Publications

http://www.japanpacific.com/english/e_translation.html

Language Translation

http://www.languagetranslation.com/contact.html

Language Line Services

http://www.languageline.com/page/careers/

Languages Unlimited

http://www.languagesunlimited.com/recr.php

Linguistic Systems Inc *http://www.linguist.com/translators.htm*

Lion Bridge *http://www.lionbridge.com/lionbridge/en-US/company/work-with-us/freelance.htm*

Multilingual Vacancies

http://www.multilingualvacancies.com/vacancies/search.php

Network Omni *http://www.networkomni.com/about-careers.asp*

Open World Multilingual Services

http://www.openworldtranslations.com/jobs.htm

Pacific Interpreters *http://www.pacificinterpreters.com/careers/*

SDL *http://www.sdl.com/en/company/careers/default.asp*

Set Systems *http://www.set-systems.com/en/contact.aspx*

Telelanguage *http://www.telelanguage.com/joinourteam.cfm*

The Linguist List *http://linguistlist.org/jobs/index.html*

Translators Café *http://translatorscafe.com/cafe/default.asp*

Ubiqus Reporting *http://www.ubiqus.com/*

UC Translations *http://www.uctranslations.com/careers.html*

We-Translate *http://www.we-translate.com/jobs.htm*

Win Translation

http://www.wintranslation.com/employment.html

Travel/Consierge

Consierge At Large (click on careers)

http://www.concierge-at-large.com/page/lopk/Contact_Us.html

VIP Desk (conierge)

http://www.vipdesk.com/info/careers_joinourteam.asp

Tutoring/ Teaching/ Education/ Homework Help

Admissions Consultants

http://www.admissionsconsultants.com/employment.asp

Aim For A Tutoring *http://www.aim4a.com/tutors.php*

American Intercontinental University

http://careers.aiuonline.edu/careers/

Berlitz Language Instructors

http://careerservices.berlitz.com/current_job_vacancies.asp

Bilingual America (Instructors)

http://www.bilingualamerica.com/about/careers/

BrainMass

http://www.brainmass.com/content/about/ota/join.php

Brainfuse *http://www.brainfuse.com/register/becomtutor.asp*

Course Bridge
http://www.coursebridge.com/html/instructor_application.asp
Creating Careers (UK) *http://www.creatingcareers.com/join-us.aspx*
Creative English Solutions (Canada)
http://www.englishsolutions.ca/ces_jobs.php?set_lang=en
Chronicle *http://chronicle.com/section/Jobs/61/*
Connections Academy
http://www.connectionsacademy.com/careers/home.aspx
CyberEdit, Inc *http://www.cyberedit.com/hub/jobs.shtml*
Dissertation Advisors *http://www.dissertationadvisors.com/*
ECOT (Substitute Teachers)
http://www.ecotohio.org/home.php?section=careers
EduWizards *http://eduwizards.com/index.php*
Electronic Classroom of Tomorrow
http://www.ecotohio.org/careers.html
ETS (click on Careers) *http://www.ets.org*
Expert Tutors *http://www.experttutors.com/employment.asp*
Explore eLearning
http://www.explorelearning.com/index.cfm?method=cCorp.dsp
Employ

Free World U (flash card writers)

http://www.freeworldu.org/static/newauthors.aspx

Global Scholar *http://www.globalscholar.com/*

Growing Stars

http://www.growingstars.com/growingstars/tutorenquiry.jsp

Homework Help

http://www.homeworkhelp.com/tutorjoinus.php

Homework Tutoring

http://*www.homeworktutoring.com/work_with_us.shtml*

Idapted *http://idapted.com/opportunities/whyjoin.html*

Kidspan *http://www.kidspan.com/career.htm*

Learners Paradise *http://www.learnersparadise.com/home/cgi-bin/homePage.pl*

Limu *http://www.limu.com/pages/teach.html*

McTutor *http://www.mctutor.com/*

NimbleMind

http://www.nimblemind.com/instructor_application_new.asp

Online Learning

http://www.onlinelearning.net/InstructorCommunity/prospectiv e.html?s=428.i090z3858.0897007830

Pearson Educational Assessment (at home scorers)

http://www.pearsonedmeasurement.com/careers/index.htm

Smart Thinking *http://www.smarthinking.com/static/e-structors/positions/*

Student Questions *http://www.studentquestions.com/faq.php*

Topics Education *http://www.topicseducation.com/about-us/about-us.cfm?content_id=25*

Tutor.com *http://www.tutor.com/apply*

Universal Class

http://www.universalclass.com/teachonline/index.htm

University of California, Berkeley Online Extension

http://learn.berkeley.edu/jobs/

Virtual University *http://vu.org/proposal.html*

Western Governers University

http://www.wgu.edu/about_WGU/employment.asp#faculty

WyzAnt *http://www.wyzant.com/tutorsignup.aspx*

Writing / Artists

Some listings in this section are job boards for writers. I have included them because they are specific resources for writers that have current jobs.

Academic Work (editors/translators)
http://www.academicword.com/emp.asp
Appingo http://www.appingo.com/contact.php
Brandon Hall *http://www.brandon-hall.com/about/about.shtml*
Beauty Care *http://www.beautycare.com/about/jobs/*
Clicknwork *http://www.clicknwork.com/opportunities/*
ComputerJobs.com (technical writing)
http://*www.technicalwriter.computerjobs.com/*
CyberEdit *http://www.cyberedit.com/hub/jobs.shtml*
Diversified Reporting
http://www.diversifiedreporting.com/job.html
EditFast *http://www.editfast.com/english/editjobs.htm*
FabJob.com *http://www.fabjob.com/jobs.html*
Freelance Writing *http://www.freelancewriting.com/*
FreeP *http://www.freep.com/legacy/jobspage/*
Fuze *http://www.ifuze.com/about/about.cfm?page=career*
Investigative Reporters and Editors *http://www.ire.org/jobs/*

Journalism Jobs

http://www.journalismjobs.com/Search_Jobs_All.cfm

Just Tech Writer Jobs *http://www.justtechwriterjobs.com/*

McMurry Copy Editor Jobs

http://jobs.copyeditor.com/home/index.cfm?site_id=502

Metaphor Studio *http://metaphorstudio.com/freelance*

Poe War *http://www.poewar.com/jobs-by-category/jobs/*

Proofread Now *http://www.proofreadnow.com/employment.htm*

Recycled Paper Greetings

http://www.recycledpapergreetings.com/artists.htm

Roman and Littlefield Publishing

http://www.rlpgbooks.com/Common/Jobs/FreelancingOpportun ities.html

Self Help Guides

http://www.selfhelpguides.com/authors_wanted.php3

Simply English Proofreading

http://www.simplyenglish.com/employment.htm

Sun Oasis *http://sunoasis.com/*

UC Berkeley Journalism Jobs

http://journalism.berkeley.edu/jobs/

Victory Productions *http://www.victoryprd.com/careers.html*

Weblogs *http://www.weblogsinc.com/*

WordFirm *http://www.wordfirm.com/employ.htm*

Writer Find *http://www.writerfind.com/*

Writing Assistance Inc *http://www.writingassist.com/jobs.html*

19903244R00063

Made in the USA
Lexington, KY
11 January 2013